The Human Body

The Muscular System

Kristin Petrie MS, RD • ABDO Publishing Company

visit us at
www.abdopublishing.com

Published by ABDO Publishing Company, 4940 Viking Drive, Edina, Minnesota 55435.

Printed in the United States.

Cover Photo: Corbis
Interior Photos: © Articulate Graphics/Custom Medical Stock Photo p. 5; Corbis pp. 1, 4, 7, 10, 11, 12, 14, 15, 21, 22, 25, 27, 29; © Educational Images/Custom Medical Stock Photo pp. 17, 19, 23; © L.Birmingham/Custom Medical Stock Photo pp. 9, 20, 24; Visuals Unlimited pp. 13, 16

Series Coordinator: Heidi M. Dahmes
Editors: Heidi M. Dahmes, Megan M. Gunderson
Art Direction: Neil Klinepier

Library of Congress Cataloging-in-Publication Data

Petrie, Kristin, 1970-
The muscular system / Kristin Petrie.
p. cm. -- (The human body)
Includes index.
ISBN-10 1-59679-711-8
ISBN-13 978-1-59679-711-6
1. Muscles--Juvenile literature. I. Title.

QM151.P48 2006
612.7'4--dc22

2005049309

Contents

Muscles Move You

Has anyone ever said to you, "Don't move a muscle!"? Usually, this means stay still when playing hide-and-seek. Just for fun, let's give it a try.

Many muscles are hard at work even when you think you are being as still as possible.

Oops, your stomach growled. That was a muscle moving. Oh no, you blinked. That was another muscle. Now you are breathing. More muscles are moving.

It is impossible to not move a muscle. Muscles are everywhere in your body. They work when you tell them to and even when you don't.

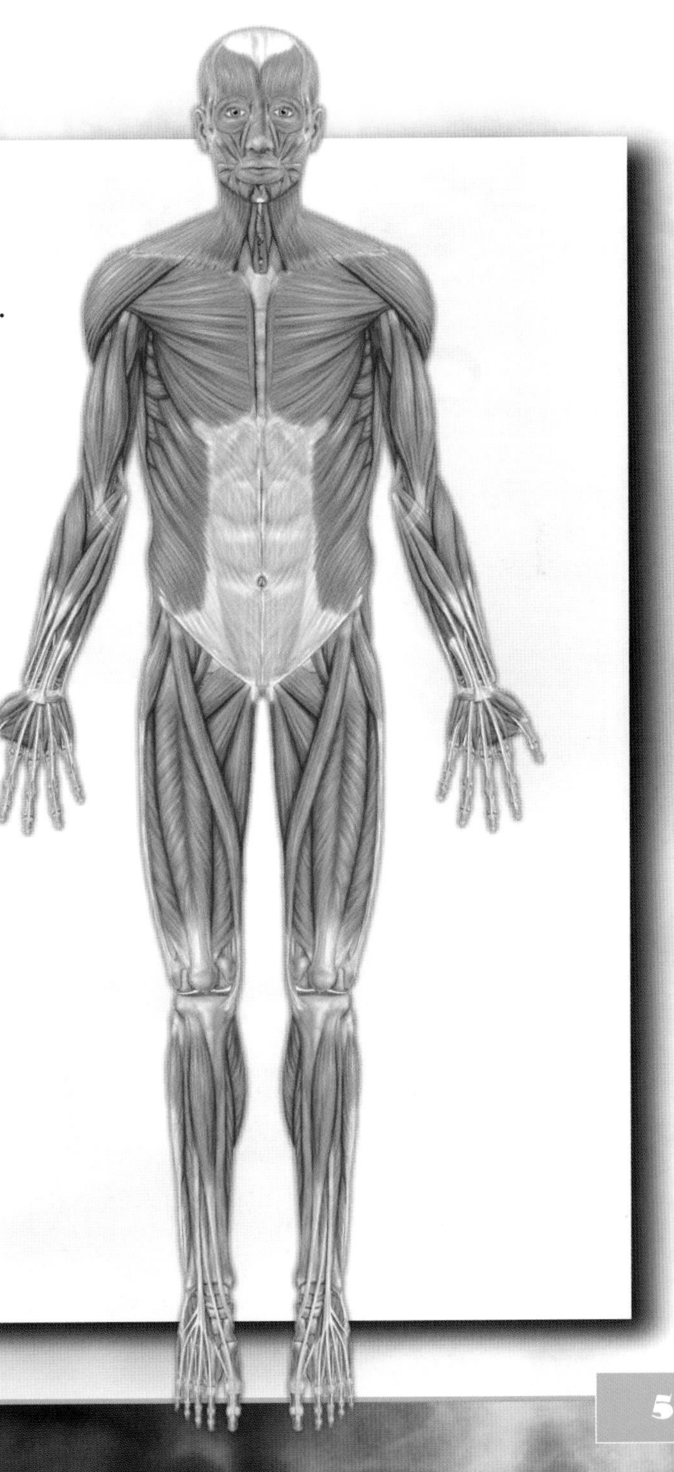

Muscles make up nearly half of an adult human's weight. Muscles are tough, elastic tissues that are responsible for all bodily functions. Even when you are sleeping, muscles are hard at work inside your body.

The Muscular System

There are more than 600 muscles in the human body. Thankfully, many of these muscles do their own thing. It would be pretty exhausting telling each of them what to do.

Can you imagine the work of bossing your muscles around? Eyes, blink. Stomach, **digest** my lunch. Keep breathing, lungs. You wouldn't have time for fun things, such as telling your leg muscles to run.

Muscles are found throughout your body. There are the muscles you can flex in your arms and legs. There are also those controlling your eyes as you read. And then, there are the small muscles in your fingers that are holding your book.

There are even muscles in places you probably weren't aware of. These include the muscles in your ear and those that make up the wall of your stomach. But let's not forget the most important muscle of all, your heart. Put them all together and you have the muscular system!

Show off those muscles! They are working hard for you.

Cardiac Muscle

There are three different types of muscle. They are cardiac, smooth, and skeletal muscle. Each type of muscle has its own important job.

Can you guess where cardiac muscle is found? The heart! It is a powerful muscle. Just think about it. Your arms and legs may grow weary after a few jumping jacks. But, your heart keeps on going. It will beat about 2 billion times during your life.

The walls of your heart are made of three layers. The outermost layer is called the pericardium. This layer is thin, but tough. It holds the heart in place while leaving room for movement. And, the pericardium has its own **lubricating** fluid. This prevents **friction** in your chest from all that beating.

Next to the pericardium is another layer called the myocardium. The myocardium's job is to relax and contract at regular **intervals**. When it relaxes, your heart fills with blood. When it contracts, blood is pumped out to all your body parts.

Just inside the myocardium is the endocardium. This layer lines the chambers of your heart. Blood swishes right up against the endocardium as it moves through this amazing muscle.

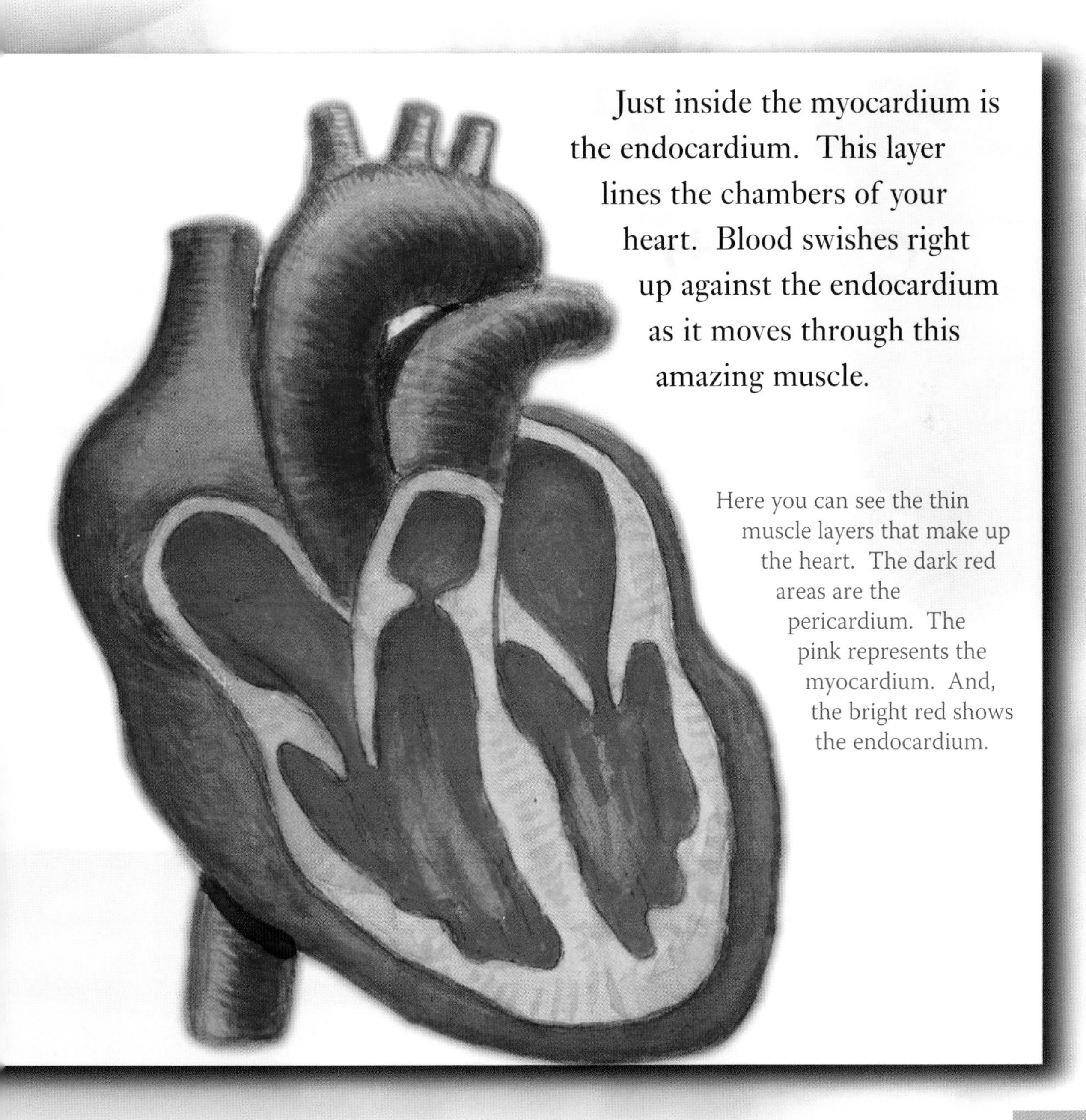

Here you can see the thin muscle layers that make up the heart. The dark red areas are the pericardium. The pink represents the myocardium. And, the bright red shows the endocardium.

Smooth Muscle

Next there are smooth muscles. We rarely think about these. This is probably because we can't flex or even see smooth muscles. Smooth muscles work on their own. For this reason, they are called involuntary muscles.

Smooth muscles make up the stuff that lies deep inside your body. The walls of your blood vessels are made of smooth muscles. And, smooth muscles are found in all of your body's hollow **organs** except for your heart.

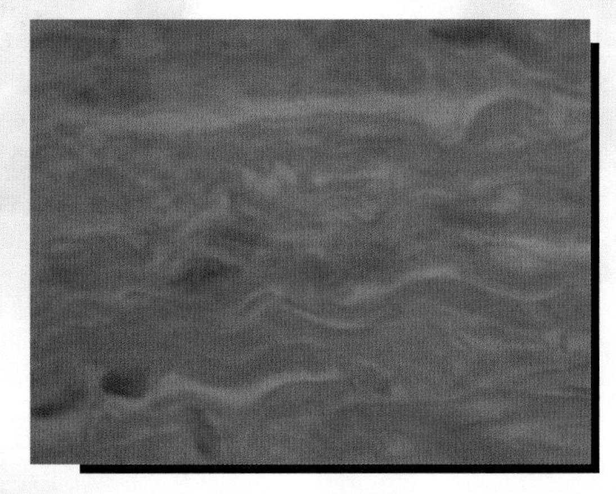

Unlike cardiac or skeletal muscle fibers, smooth muscle tissue is not striated, or striped.

Let's not forget two very important organs. The walls of your stomach and intestines are made of smooth muscle. When you hear your stomach growl, you'll know it's smooth muscle talking! This means it needs more fuel.

Hunger pangs are the contractions of your stomach wall. These occur when your body doesn't have enough fuel to work on!

Skeletal Muscle

A deltoid muscle moves each of your shoulders. So, you are able to do things such as swing a bat.

The third type of muscle is called skeletal muscle. This is what you show off when someone tells you to flex. But, skeletal muscles aren't just for show. They help you chew your lunch, wave to your friends, and sprint for the bus.

Skeletal muscles come in many shapes and sizes. Some of the large ones help you walk or lift objects. But, smaller skeletal muscles are just as important. Tiny muscles in your pinkie help you type and clean your ears! And, muscles in your little toe help you stay balanced.

Skeletal muscles are made of fibers bundled together. Some of these fibers are up to 12 inches (31 cm) long.

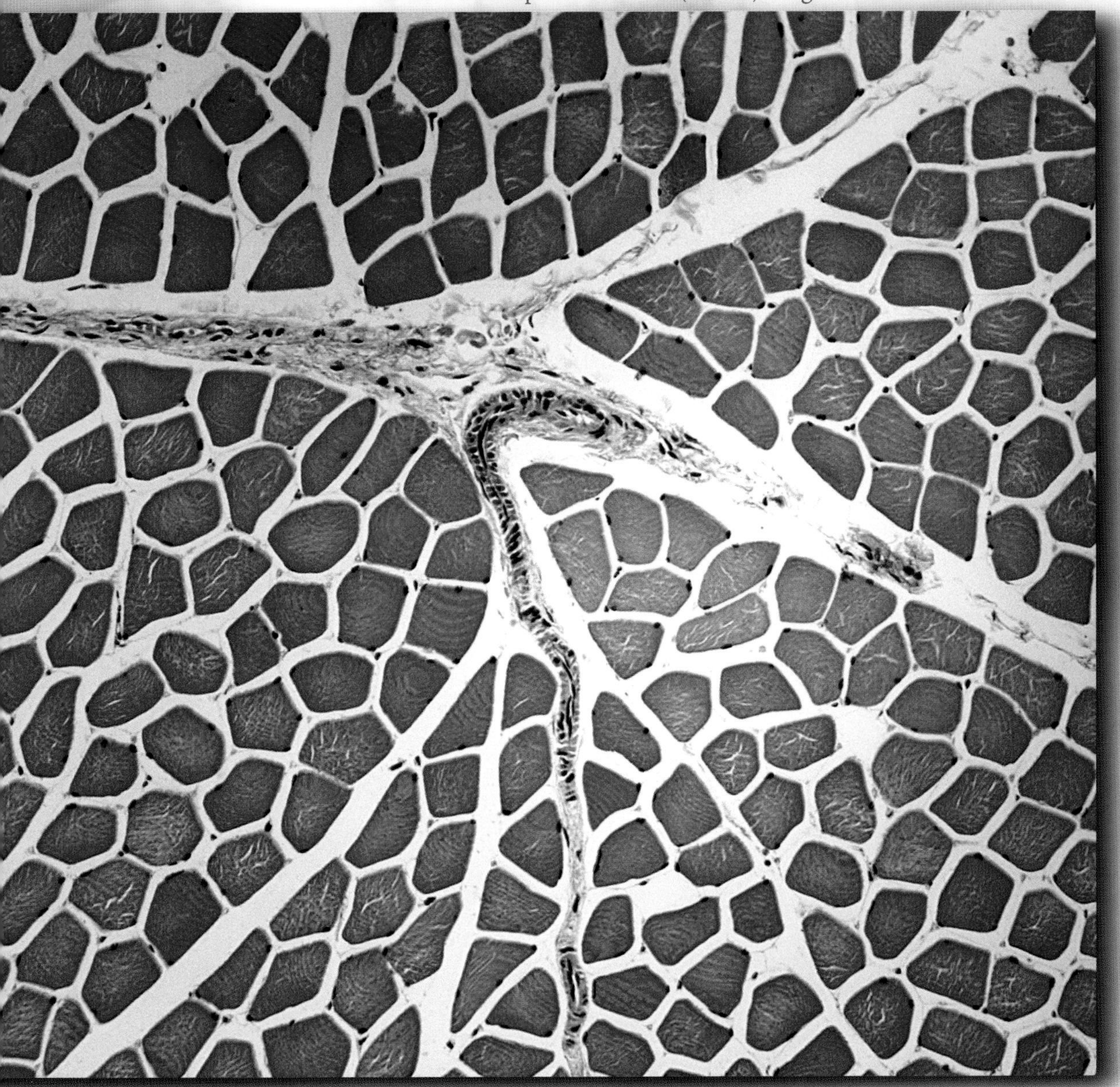

Skeletal muscles control our facial expressions. Some people believe that frowning uses more muscles than smiling. However, this is not known for sure. So keep smiling!

Every one of your muscles has its own name. Some are named by their function. Muscles that bend a limb are called flexors. Muscles that straighten a limb are called extensors. Elbow flexors and extensors are working as you bend and straighten your arms.

Other muscles can swing a limb to the side, away from the body. These are abductors. Those muscles that move a limb sideways toward your body are adductors. The muscles at your hips are good examples. They are called hip abductors and hip adductors.

Still other muscles are named by their shape, size, or location. Your back muscle is named for its shape. This four-sided muscle is called the trapezius because it is shaped like a trapezoid. Your gluteus maximus received its name because of its size. *Maximus* means "large."

All of your skeletal muscles have two things in common. They must be connected to something else to have power and strength. And, they move when you tell them to. For this reason, they are called voluntary muscles.

The brain and the spinal cord tell skeletal muscles to contract. Exercise will keep your muscles in shape.

Muscle Power

Even a superhero's big muscles would be useless if they weren't attached to something. So, some of your muscles are connected to your skin. Many of your muscles are attached to your bones. Together, skeletal muscles and bones give your body power.

Your voluntary muscles, bones, and **ligaments** make up the musculoskeletal system. Most skeletal muscles are attached directly to your bones. Strong bands called **tendons** hold them together. Tendons are cords of tough tissue. They turn your bones into **levers**. When you contract a muscle, the tendon pulls the attached bone with it.

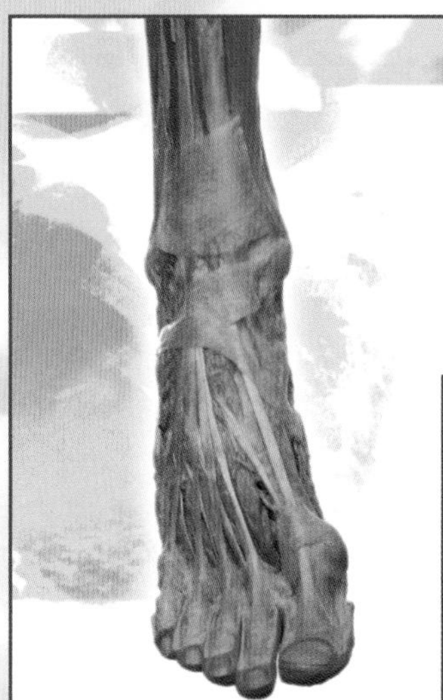

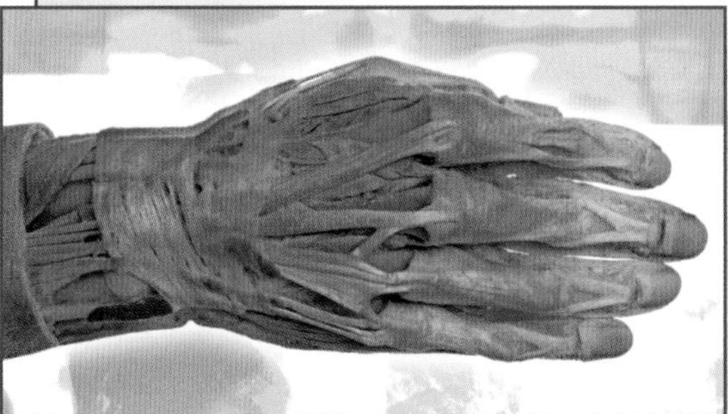

Muscles and tendons

Flex your biceps muscle in your upper arm. Notice that flexing makes the muscle shorter. How does that work? At one end, the biceps is attached to your shoulder. At the other end, it connects to your lower arm bones. When you flex, the muscle shortens and pulls your lower arm upward. Now you can show off your biceps!

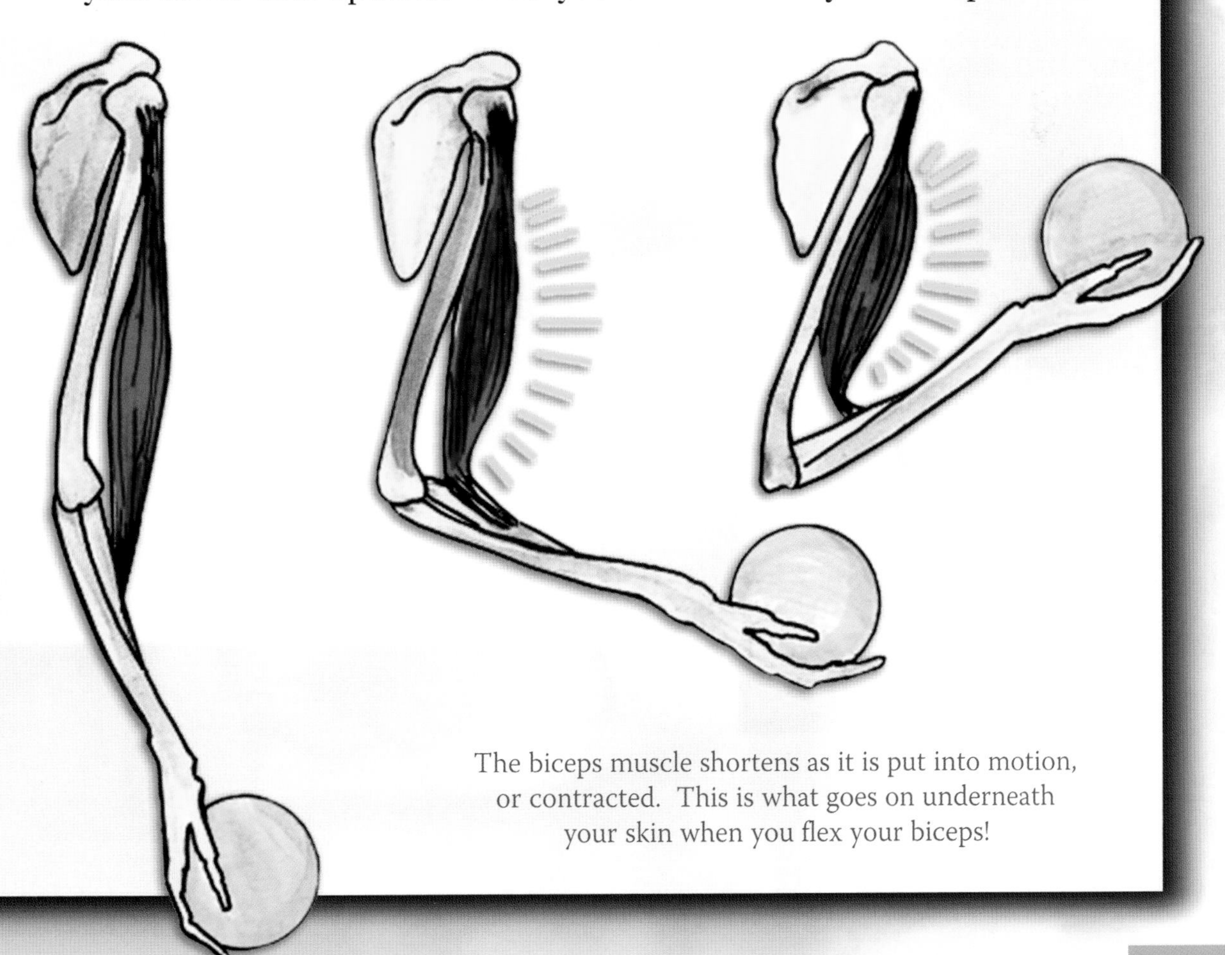

The biceps muscle shortens as it is put into motion, or contracted. This is what goes on underneath your skin when you flex your biceps!

What Muscles Are Made Of

Every muscle in your body is made up of a huge number of cells. These cells are also called muscle fibers. There are three types of muscle cell. Each kind is **specialized** for its role in the body.

Cardiac muscle cells are rectangular. Each cell has one nucleus. Cardiac muscle cells are striated and branched. These branches connect them to surrounding cells. The branching fibers allow nerve impulses to pass from cell to cell.

Smooth muscle cells are spindle shaped. They are wide in the middle with tapered ends. The cells lace together to form smooth sheets. And like cardiac cells, each smooth muscle cell has one nucleus.

Opposite page: Cardiac muscle cells *(top)* are striated. Smooth muscle cells *(below)* are not. But both are involuntary.

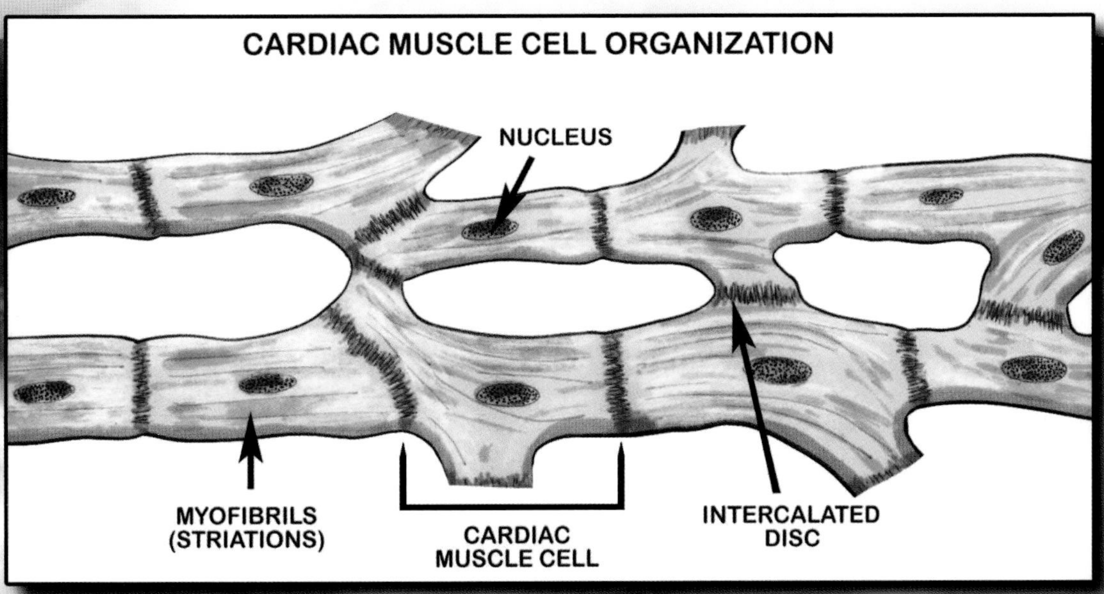
CARDIAC MUSCLE CELL ORGANIZATION
NUCLEUS
MYOFIBRILS
(STRIATIONS)
CARDIAC
MUSCLE CELL
INTERCALATED
DISC

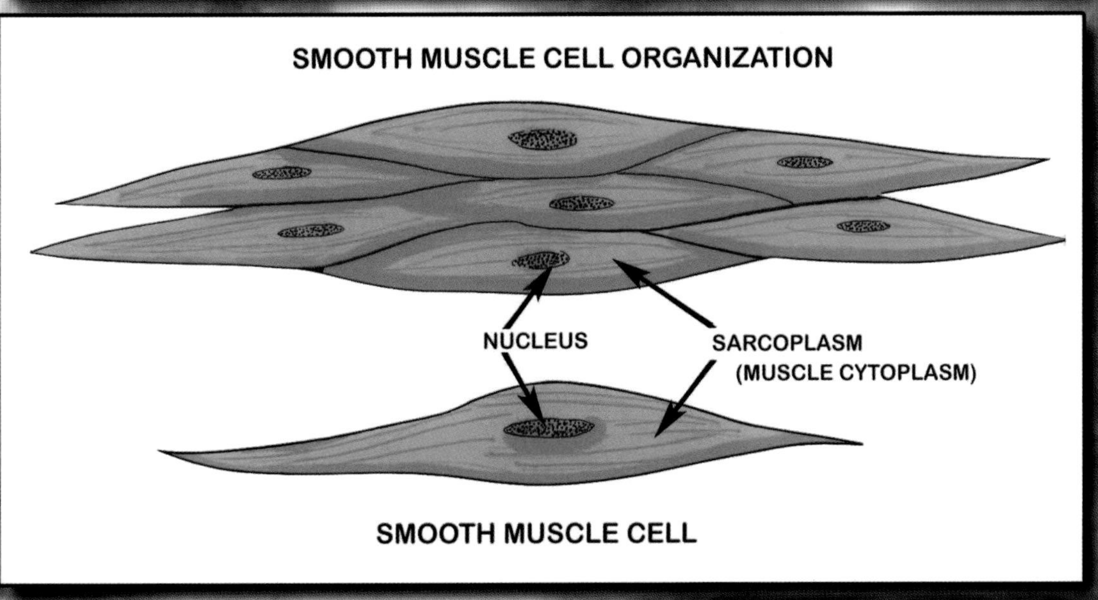
SMOOTH MUSCLE CELL ORGANIZATION
NUCLEUS
SARCOPLASM
(MUSCLE CYTOPLASM)
SMOOTH MUSCLE CELL

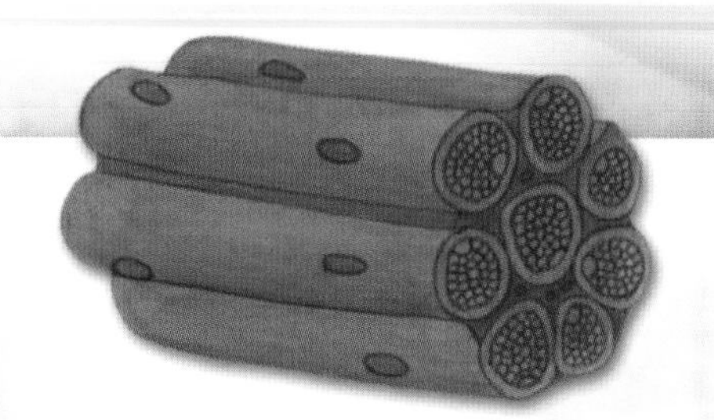

Skeletal muscle fibers are longer and shaped like logs. They have many nuclei. Some fibers are very long. Look down at your leg. The fibers that make up your thigh muscles extend from the top of your leg down over your knee.

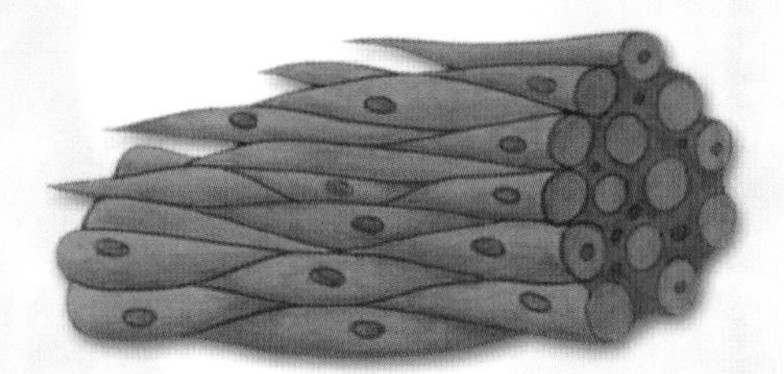

Skeletal muscles are further divided into two types of fibers. The first type is called fast twitch. Fast twitch fibers are big and contract quickly. They give your muscles quick bursts of energy. You use fast twitch fibers for activities that require a short burst of strength. These include sprinting and lifting a weight.

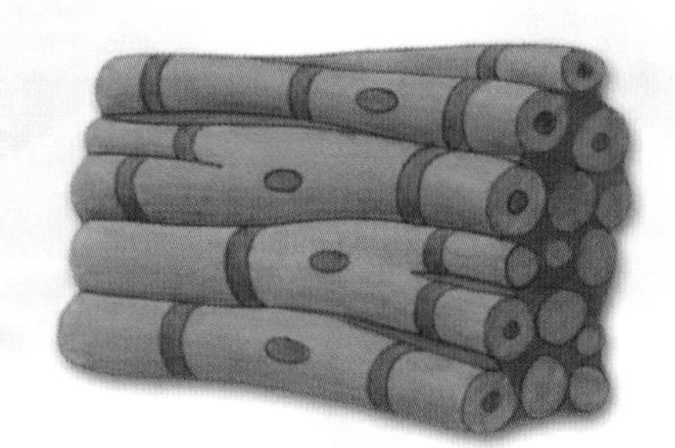

(Top to bottom) Skeletal, smooth, and cardiac muscle

The second type of skeletal muscle fiber is called slow twitch. These fibers provide longer-lasting energy. Can you guess when slow twitch fibers are working for you? Endurance activities, such as distance walking and running, require the use of these fibers.

Everyone has a blend of fast and slow twitch fibers. Slow twitch fibers work for a longer period of time. This boy is using fast twitch fibers, which tire easily.

VOLUNTARY MUSCLES

Voluntary muscles move when we want them to. Skeletal muscles are voluntary muscles. You use skeletal muscles when you kick a soccer ball or jump into a pool.

Quadriceps are the muscles on the front of the thighs. Playing sports such as soccer strengthens these muscles.

The triceps muscle contracts to pull the forearm bones, while the biceps muscle relaxes. This is how you straighten your arm.

Your brain sends messages to voluntary muscles through motor nerves. Want to raise your hand? Your brain shoots a signal down a motor nerve to your arm. A bunch of muscles there get the message. They work together to shoot your arm into the air.

Voluntary muscles work in pairs. When one muscle contracts, the other muscle relaxes. To move your arm, the muscle on one side pulls your arm bone to lift up. The muscle on the other side pulls to reach down.

Simple voluntary actions such as waving your hand don't take much thought. This is because your brain and nerves have memorized the action. Through practice, even voluntary muscle actions become natural.

When the biceps muscle contracts, it pulls the forearm bones up, while the triceps muscle relaxes. This is how you bend your arm.

Involuntary Muscles

Involuntary muscles work on their own. You don't have to do a thing. What a relief! Cardiac and smooth muscles are involuntary muscles.

Unlike voluntary muscles, we are usually unaware of our involuntary muscle contractions. For example, your heart muscles are

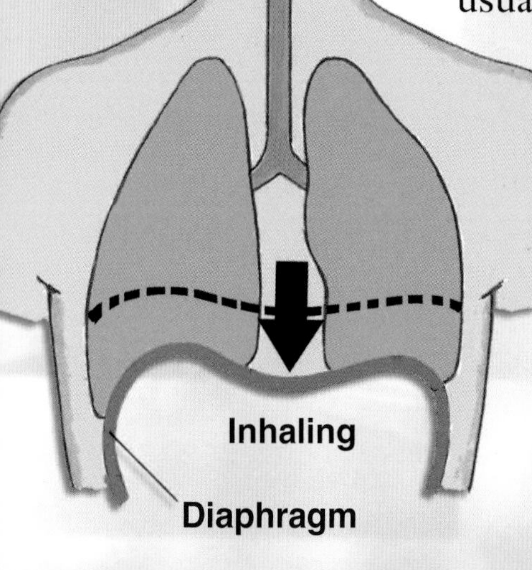

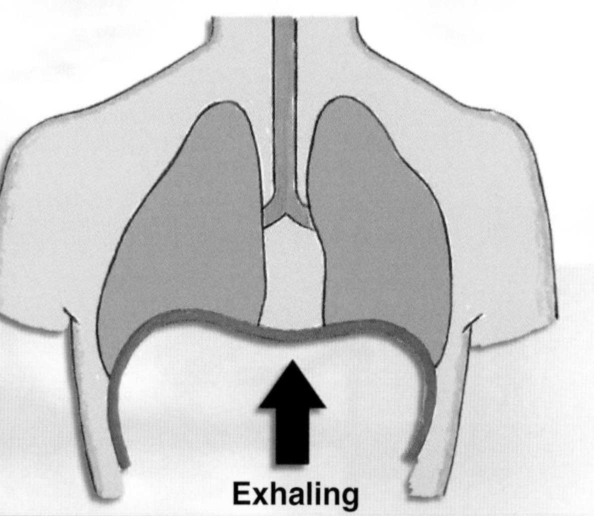

Smooth muscles are involved in breathing, too. These muscles regulate airflow through the lungs.

Smooth muscles also control the size of your pupils in bright light.

contracting constantly. More involuntary muscles move blood along your vessels. And, the muscles in your eyelids make you blink regularly so your eyeballs don't dry out.

Sometimes your involuntary muscles make themselves known. Have you ever been sick and thrown up? Your smooth muscles were at work. They pushed your food out of your stomach, up through your esophagus, and out of your mouth.

Diseases

The term muscular dystrophy is used for any one of a group of muscle diseases. These diseases cause muscles to become weak and slowly waste away. People who suffer from muscular dystrophy may become **paralyzed**.

Multiple sclerosis (MS) is a nervous system disease. But it affects muscle control. In MS patients, nerves that send messages to muscles become damaged. The muscles do not receive their signals. This causes them to become weak.

Guess what? There is something that causes everyone's muscles to break down. It's called aging. But with regular exercise, you can help your muscles stay healthy.

Some people use medications to help manage their muscle disease. And, some have special instruments or wheelchairs to help them get around. People who suffer from muscular diseases want to be just like everyone else. So, treat everyone you meet as a friend!

Opposite page: Researchers are working hard to fight against muscular dystrophy. They test mice and other animals to find cures for muscular illnesses.

Keeping Muscles Healthy

There are several ways to keep your muscles happy. They like a workout. Whether you are swimming or skipping, exercise keeps muscles in shape.

Strong muscles are less likely to get hurt. They also burn more calories. This helps your body stay strong and healthy. Weak muscles cause many problems, including back pain and weight gain.

Eating a variety of nutritious foods is important for keeping your muscles happy. Muscles need food for making energy. They need vitamins and minerals to help them respond to nerve signals. And, muscles need **nutrients** to grow and repair themselves.

Pick your foods wisely. For example, a banana gives your muscles potassium. Potassium regulates the amount of water in your muscles. A glass of milk provides calcium and protein. These are both necessary for proper growth. Remember to treat your muscles well. They'll keep you going!

Work out with your friends. It's fun and good for you!

GLOSSARY

digest - to break down food into substances small enough for the body to absorb.

friction - the rubbing of one object against another.

interval - time or space between two events or things.

lever - a rigid piece that sends and modifies force or motion from one point to another while rotating about a fixed point.

ligament - a band of strong tissue that connects two bones or cartilages or holds a body organ in place.

lubricant - a substance, such as grease, used to reduce friction between moving parts.

nutrient - a substance found in food and used in the body to promote growth, maintenance, and repair.

organ - a part of an animal or a plant that is composed of several kinds of tissues and that performs a specific function. The heart, liver, gallbladder, and intestines are organs of an animal.

paralyze - to cause a loss of motion or feeling in a part of the body.

specialize - to adapt or limit to a specific purpose or use.

tendon - a band of tough fibers that joins a muscle to another part, such as a bone.

Saying It

dystrophy - DIHS-truh-fee

esophagus - ih-SAH-fuh-guhs

gluteus maximus - GLOO-tee-uhs MAK-suh-muhs

musculoskeletal - muhs-kyuh-loh-SKEH-luh-tuhl

sclerosis - skluh-ROH-suhs

striated - STREYE-ay-tuhd

trapezius - truh-PEE-zee-uhs

Web Sites

To learn more about the muscular system, visit ABDO Publishing Company on the World Wide Web at **www.abdopub.com**. Web sites about the human body are featured on our Book Links page. These links are routinely monitored and updated to provide the most current information available.

INDEX